A C
R

Kate Foley

ARACHNE PRESS
2018

First published in UK 2018 by Arachne Press Limited
100 Grierson Road, London SE23 1NX
www.arachnepress.com
© Arachne Press 2018
ISBN: 978-1-909208-53-7

The moral rights of the author have been asserted
All content is copyright the author.

All rights reserved. This book is sold subject to the condition that it shall not by way of trade or otherwise, be lent, resold, hired out or otherwise circulated without the publisher's prior written consent in any form or binding or cover other than that in which it is published and without similar condition including this condition being imposed on the subsequent purchaser.
Except for short passages for review purposes no part of this publication may be reproduced, stored in a retrieval system or transmitted in any form, or by any means, electronic, mechanical, photocopying, recording or otherwise without prior written permission of Arachne Press.
Printed on wood free paper in the UK by TJ International, Padstow.

Poems collected here previously appeared as follows
Quail Syndrome in Soft Engineering Onlywomen Press 1994

Here's The Church Where's The Steeple in A Year Without Apricots Blackwater Press 1999

From The Silver Rembrandt, in The Silver Rembrandt, Shoestring Press 2008

Sleeping Together in Laughter from the Hive Shoestring Press, 2004

Heart Surgery, In the Dog Watches and *To the Field Of Reeds* in One Window North, Shoestring Press, 2012

Foreigners in the international magazine Versal 12

Mothers and Fathers in The Don't Touch Garden Arachne Press 2015

Jailbreak in Liberty Tales Arachne Press 2017

Kate Foley is a widely published, prize-winning poet who has read in many UK and European locations. Her first collection, *Soft Engineering,* was short listed for best first collection at Aldeburgh.

Her working life has ranged from delivering babies to conserving delicate archaeological material. She became Head of English Heritage's scientific and technical research laboratories. Although she has always written poetry it wasn't until she gave up the day job that she began to publish more widely.

She now lives with her wife between Amsterdam and Suffolk, where she performs, writes, edits, leads workshops and whenever possible works with artists in other disciplines.

A Gift of Rivers is her eighth full collection.

Some of these poems were first collected and privately printed in a monograph as a birthday gift for Kate's wife, Tonnie, with the help of Jeremy Greenwood.

Also by Kate Foley from Arachne Press:
The Don't Touch Garden (available as print and audio)

CONTENTS

Permission	7
Wishbone	8
Catechisms	9
A Loose Configuration	16
A Little Local Love	17
Like a Glove	18
Ordinary Exile	19
Foreigners	20
Mothers and Fathers	22
Unmasked	23
From The Silver Rembrandt	24
Sticks	26
Becoming Enough	27
The Quail Syndrome	28
Jailbreak	29
Sheep May Safely	30
Here's The Church Where's The Steeple	32
Back to Basics	34
A Gift Of Rivers	35
Wives	36
When I Lie Next To You In Sleep	38
I am Your Second Language	40
In The Dog Watches	41
Sleeping Together	42
Heart Surgery	44
To the Field Of Reeds	46

for Tonnie

PERMISSION

Don't need permission,
not from god,
any god,
even She,
not the Virgin,
(though soft spot conceded),
not the nuns,
starched into their icing-
sugar knickers –
('...you wouldn't want to do something *unfresh*!')
not the dove,
who never turned up
when the Bishop said he would,
not priests, politicians, Public
Opinion – not even Mum,
though I wished she'd Come Out
and admitted she knew.

Don't need permission – only,
yours,
and hardest of all,
from a place I never
visited before,
from me,
to love you.

WISHBONE

'Make me a poet' I say quietly
to the small torn knuckle of gristle
and bone I've won.

More 'poetic' to wish on the evening star
that comes out whether or not you're there
to see. My bone's

torn from the delicate vee
your fingers fish from the washing up.
As we pull it quivers

with the unspoken weight of wishes, yours
and mine. Is poetry to speak what can't be said
or catch its fugitive shape in a net of words?

I lick my fingers and the silent
salt speaks its sharpness
to my lips.

CATECHISMS

i   Who made You?

***Who** made you?* ***God** made me.*
***Why** did God make me?* Little girl
voices, piercing as a chalk squeak, filling
late autumn's afternoon classroom dusk,
believing in the importance of themselves
chanting. Like ***all****intergethergirls*, ***this***
fineweathergirls, knowing if you dropped
the rhythm, made the rope stutter, something
that hung between you might break. Snap
of a brass switch. Shadows run from Mother
Monica's habit. Worn soap, no longer ivory,
her face in the scrimped, yellow 40 watt glimmer,
is like all mothers' thinking abstractedly of tea,
can't or won't tell the big secret I know
she knows, *Who or Why or **How** I must be?*

ii   The Means of Grace

Pamela Grierson wasn't even a Catholic.
She had tight fair baby curls – you could
unkindly say a frizz – and small teeth
which would age grey, not yellow but
Mother St Helen, whose teeth were already
yellow and Mother Aquinas, whose farmer's
face reddened as she looked fondly, knew
despite being a Prod, she could do no wrong.
'Original Justice' that state is called and wangles Noble
Savages and Prods whom Providence has excluded
from the Means of Grace, into Heaven. 'Why?'
I argued. 'She's here at school. Invincible Ignorance!'
A mean, ungraceful choice of weapon. The sin
of logic over kindness. It will always win.

iii   And the Hope of Glory

which gathered at the door of the chapel
in febrile silence, in the splash of holy water
on your dress, in the thin, wobbly voices of nuns,
and the shadows round the blaze of white and gold,
Himself, who never failed to disappoint.
But the old, brown gardening nun who swallowed
and smiled as I cut her irises to the corm,
then showed me the folded purple thrust and green
that has to grow, knew skill, weather, luck
and kindness, all as strands of hope,
the ontology of her garden not
what it seemed but twisted together,
rough and strong as twine
supporting scarlet runners or a vine.

iv   For Four out of Seven Sacraments

you get a white dress, well I suppose
in a mother and baby home they lend
you one. Late to communion, wouldn't
wear a sash, suffered rag curlers, skew-
whiff wreath, no spectacles, sun blazing off
the shiny serge bellies of the marching band,
Our Lady's grotto a white blur. Confirmation –
legs longer, dress shorter, pink bishop's hand
and waiting, waiting for that friendly
fat pigeon who never came, to light on
my shoulder, nibble my ear. Somewhere
in that gap between dry host and absent
bird, I knew the fourth white dress would be
a lie too far, even for me.

v   The Blessed Sacrament

leprechaun-sized in its unleavened waistcoat
hummed in its box. They changed its curtains
to purple for thinking about sin, white when you had to
rejoice and green when you could relax a bit,
housewifely nuns tending their sacred crumb.
When I whistled, *Go and tell Our Blessed Lord
what you've done*, said Mother. Exposed mid-morning
to the force-field of the tabernacle my hunted eyes
fell upon the strawberry bosom of Jesus,
was He behind the curtains,too? OK – *whistling, smelling
Our Lady's flowers, passing my beetroot
To Stella Jump* …but the one I could never tell?
How to resist the dangerous pull of Jesus in his small box,
doughty as a bee, fumbling my heart's locks?

vi   Mortal Sin

had only to do with the bits of bible
we mustn't look at or know too much about
but trust Our Lady to keep you clean
and learn about rabbits in formalin
and eggs, of course and not touch the sacred
host in your mouth but if it gets stuck
on the roof, scrape it off delicately with your
tongue, not enjoying it, and keep your top button
done up, even in summer, and never, never
touch. How can you swallow without spit?
Not touch without kindness
fleeing your soul? Lady, protect me
from the sin of frost. That mortal flaw
needing the salvation of fertile dirt to thaw.

vii   But my Guardian Angel

came swinging easily through
the chapel roof, only touching lightly
the frilly wrought iron lamp stanchions,
ducking her chrysanthemum head past toothpaste
excrescences of Gothic and landing with a whump
of powerful thighs on the wedding cake altar.
Wings creaked like sea-going yachts. The pink
and azure Virgin turned her head, fractionally,
widened her eyes. My angel looked at me, grinned,
and a sudden wind ruffled my hair, under
my pudding hat. All that dead hush, smelling of nuns'
clothes, washed in yellow soap, used incense,
pious effort, swept up by feathers, like floor
dust through a blue, suddenly opened door.

A LOOSE CONFIGURATION

Which bit goes where?
How will I know?

Bad enough
you must wear special clothes –

are you Butch? are you Femme? eh? which? –
and worse, you must take them off!

Don't worry, when it's time to shed,
you'll slide like a buttonless snakeskin,

your careful assembled self a vulnerable
scatter on the floor.

Now you are a loose configuration
of moving parts, like a scramble

of wild brambles in a soft wind.
Thorns forgotten,

your prehensile tongue
finds the darkest fruit.

A LITTLE LOCAL LOVE

How much is enough?
A crumb for a mouse,
a crust for a child?

All the blanched
and broken footprints
of the world

cry 'more!' and all the empty
hands print their lifeline
on your conscience.

So they should,
your better self agrees.
Let your heart remain unbroken

so your hand
can find your pocket!
Sometimes all we can manage

is a little local love,
your cold toes on my warm skin.

LIKE A GLOVE

When I put on your body
like a glove we flex and cry,
our limbs knotted together,
our skins shedding

their fragrant cells, our hearts
harbouring that slow icicle
whose melt you may not halt
if love's to wash all permafrosted

history clean. Once thawed, we'll know
whose heart stands where, each
leaning against the other, but clear.
I shall see agape,

transparent as a window,
shine through Eros, its shadows
and burning mixed on your face –
how it redeems the solitary myth of bone.

ORDINARY EXILE

Home is not only where the heart is.
Sometimes that scuffed organ
cries 'Let me out!'

We are not the Roma in the street,
our beautiful hands bent
to cup small denomination coins.

If we beg – and we try not to –
it is only by the slightest narrowing
of our eyes to bring closer

that freckle of green shadow from a late
spring, this crust, edged with light
on a blue-white plate.

The tender inside of an elbow
is the ordinary exile
we long to touch.

Dailiness roosts like a great
black hen on the frail perch
of our believing

that there is somewhere
a little space for us
smelling of feathers.

FOREIGNERS

A flock of parakeets swaggers
across this window,
green leaves uncurling.

We're not supposed to like them.
They elbow out the sparrows,
small brown truffles,

chipper, street-wise,
knowing how to charm
but no defence

against the shiv in their backs,
from the careless, easy-come,
flash-green spivs.

How to be human,
to put a hand on the scales
that balances must and should,

to love the foreign,
the different, the strange,
while keeping

a hollow alive
in our hearts,
for that lost brown ball,

all our sparrows?

See how that exotic green lights up
the empty, dun winter sky.

MOTHERS AND FATHERS

A very wise poet once said lovers
'are each other's parents'.

I don't think you're my father,
that puzzled, gentle, blunt-handed

man. Maybe you occupy the space
where touch might have been skin

and feeding nurture? Your
hands smell of leaves, compost

and piano keys.
Time to play

mothers and fathers again,
to say 'table' and 'bed'

and 'house' but mothered
and fathered at last,

let the roof shelter
        nouns into verbs.

UNMASKED

This is my eye mask
called spectacles.

This is my face mask
for showing who you are.

This is my mask of soft grey fur
for being polite.

This is my child mask.
I didn't wear it long.

This is my bird mask.
It doesn't really fit.

This is my love mask
and these are my fingers.

Do I need gloves?

From THE SILVER REMBRANDT

'She's licking my ear!'
Slow as cooling molasses
in the fag-end of Saturday night, after the heaving
and jumping of *Yellow Submarine*, the juke box spools out
Strangers in the Night.

Lily feels that tiny rough
wetness sample her ear,
watches through half shut eyes,
women bending to women,
carnal and rich as the Song of Solomon.

                          She is drunk –
on her first sight of Smithy,
the bartender, all muscle and fat and oiled quiff,
packed into her checked suit,
on the women,
with turned back cuffs, sharp flared jeans,
on the rhapsodical, raffish noise,
on the visiting man with big-haired wig,
lipstick, and huge, high-heeled feet,
on the elderly lesbians, in lambswool sweaters,
wearing sensible shoes, holding hands,
on the queasy sense of homesickness,
at a frontier crossed,
but not yet home.

                        'Shall we go?' asks Frances.
Lily's lips try to form a 'no'. She nods.
Somewhere out of sight her guardian cockerel
gives a faint, triumphant crow.

All the risible imperfections
and awkwardness of first-time sex
cluster round their bed –

for Lily, no toothbrush, the way their teeth
clash till they become acquainted,
an accidental fart,

the cat, who, jealous, jumps
on Frances' back with macho claws,
but under, over all, the miracle

of skin, blooming, where words can't,
double-sided, wrapping without,
within, lining every orifice
with soft light...

STICKS

Who I was is not who I am.
This is how we used to do it

when I was who I was.
If I could say, two dry sticks

rubbed together – but you still have
small green scars where leaves will come.

Who do you see when you look
so closely? Once I lusted

after a fat girl with whiskers
so I know shabby skin is OK

and the rest of a tired body with its smells
bagged up in it – but now the bear fat

of a long winter is melting
the dormouse is coming out of its teapot

but it's clear that spring can't be done,
something more than the kindness

of animals is needed. Something
able to love the mutability of water.

Please wait for the clouds
that have hibernated in my eyes.

BECOMING ENOUGH

For one brief instant
every week – it may
be every month -
I am content
with all I never dared,
who I never was,
who I have become

or am becoming.

Thank you, I say,
to no-one in particular.
Thank you for the arrhythmia
of time that pulses light,
so the beloved particularity
of moments is a backlit,
sudden choreography

of enough.

THE QUAIL SYNDROME

They pair when their breast bars match,
like iron filings to the magnet –
strong lines of force,

snatch of like to like.
How the earth and tides pull
is in the mixture.

What chance has love
subverted by attraction?
The cure is hard.

Debar the nest; breast shaped
simple curve for a few
warm eggs.

Make each bird
take to its untried wings;
stake its life on air.

JAIL BREAK *on not speaking enough Dutch*

I have made a little prison for myself.
Outside words fall from the trees
like apples.

The newsreader folds his face
in planes of sorrow. Who
is being carried out in that black bag?

Not everything is hidden.
There is always the language of lips
that conjugates harmony

of bed and table
and a language of hands
where tenderness lies in the stroke

of the fine hairs
on our separate skins.
But isn't it time for a jail break?

Shall I pray to myself to find my legs?
to let myself out? I won't shoot my jailer –
we've known each other far too long –

no. We'll join hands and run
like rabbits over the free grass
that speaks in tongues

and shout irregular verbs.

SHEEP MAY SAFELY

Grazing past each other
pastured in the long open
meadows of our pleasure

where we may safely
laugh with the silky dog
who herds tall, harebell clouds,

I taste your folded salt,
my fingers rouged
with the rose petal brown

of your blood's dying
and stare with pupils
vertical as its own

into the rough agate dare
of that brindled mask,
our haunting and our dark.

Yellow eyed terminator,

nothing
will make you kind
or domestic

but lie down in our field
for a while and let us get used to the sun
smell in your rough coat.

HERE'S THE CHURCH, WHERE'S THE STEEPLE?

How do I know your hands
tell me the truth? Because
mine cannot lie.

Stripped of carefulness
in the strong disinfectant of truth
they're naked, no longer ready

for easy, familiar gestures,
for wooing or soothing
when they should fall silent in my lap.

When your hand crept cold,
sweaty, trembling, into mine,
no words were said,

but mine, trembling back,
confirmed the invitation.
Your hands are limber,

nimble, good at making
gothic steeples,
while mine make roman arches,

but used to the last resource
of touch, each neuron fired,
fingers speaking in tongues,

our hands lie, resting quietly
after the work of love,
in the earned interlace of silence.

BACK TO BASICS

Sometimes when our only link is skin
I want to take it off, walk naked
in my bones.

Feel this – tapping the mount of skull –
kiss me here – and here. Mouth space
and pubic arch are wry with shadow.

All the unfound words
spill from a well behind my eyes.
Abscission clicks as letters and digits

scissored from meaning float
in an unspooled algebraic ribbon
for space to resolve.

Deprived of the comfort of skin, its illusion
of old silk, its partial osmosis,
its incontinent leak of tenderness,

how can you do tender? How heart? How find
the place where godless, skinless, heartless
moving is moving still?

A GIFT OF RIVERS

Flying into Amsterdam
I see how a giant comb has pulled the hairs of the fields
into straight, wet lines, how the occasional hedge
runs on wiry feet away from the open,
                              how as the plane tilts
the edge of the water-land-water seems ghostly as the meniscus
an empty glass has left behind,
                              how the many transparent
voices of water thicken in canals
and the old windows in the city
are so like rolled water you wait for fish
to swim through their bubbles.

When I left the branches across our yard
were empty. Now small green fists
punch out space.

Thank you for your gift of rivers.

WIVES

There are not many wives
of women yet,
even in Amsterdam.

You'd think,
wouldn't you,
that someone so careful

of her image as me,
or so equable she doesn't
need to be, like you,

would be, if not
politically correct, at least
aware of the irony.

That tragi-comic state,
stained bed-sheets, barter
and annexation.

Yet we did the whole lot,
except cake, and our wedding
photos show the same raw

transparent grins as bridals
do and everyone cried
at your brother's speech

and I for one am too
tired after a lifetime
of weights and measures

to do more than crawl
between our uxorious sheets
for a little private poetry.

So wife, whose wife I am,
be pleased by this title made innocent
by the kindly burghers of Amsterdam.

WHEN I LIE NEXT TO YOU IN SLEEP

I remember that at precisely 5.38pm you gave me
a wire basket at the supermarket.
Thank you, I said, very politely.

You *did* look familiar. I know
when I lie beside all the long length
of you that you're not the woman

from the DSS, or my mother,
or god forbid, my father
and I have never forgotten

your mother-tongue, though
in daylight it goes up in smoke.
I don't need you to remind me

that we were once very young –
though never together –
since the heat of your thigh

and the weight of your arm
stir deep shadows
in the courtyards of sleep.

When you next come in from the garden
smelling of earth and sweat,
I swear

from the deepest well
of my most truthful dream,
I shall remember you.

I AM YOUR SECOND LANGUAGE

Your first, as in mother-tongue
stroked you in your cot, rocked you
in your father's arms, gentled
you when you grazed your knee,
sang from your mother's oma fiets,
followed you to school, scratched
your own name on the blackboard,
taught you your lover's hands,
the inlets of her body, how
language is not simple speech
but song
>
> and how our stories
> written in salt,
> anagrams of faith and unfaith
> refuse to make a pattern.

Brave, then, to choose a second language
to be the grammar of your bed and table.

IN THE DOGWATCHES

You are lying in your sleepboat,
back keel-up towards me,
knee from your fallen leg
deep in the bed,
one sunken arm turned
at elbow and wrist,
so I see your fimbriated fingers,
fluttering in the floorcloth grey of 3 o'clock.

Suddenly your wrist hinges,
fingers snap crabshut
on your shoulder.

You whimper softly.
What is this old dog
dream you are in?

Discreetly I lick the three knobs
of your spine level with my nose
so you feel puppied.

You heave yourself face-flat
with a collapsing harrump
of shingle
as the waves come back in.

SLEEPING TOGETHER

Our bodies chattering quietly together
like starlings, prepare
as each cell settles on the branches of our sleep.

We are used to this now, no longer find
a ripe fart or sour morning breath an embarrassment,
or passion an interruption,

any more than a floating crisp packet
disrupts the flow of broad water.
You lay your head in the hollow of my arm-pit.

Time's up. Now comes the small animal
shuffle of turning, breast to back,
belly to buttocks

and later in the conversation that velcro
kiss of sweating skin
unsticking

and a brief pause for the cooler reaches
of sleep. 'What did you dream?', you ask.
You felt my hand heavy as a small anchor

on your thigh and briefly our boat
rocked with a small shock
outside of language. If growing old

is giving up what you know you can say,
then not only our days aquire patina.
Our nights deepen transparently.

Our speech, like a mute swan's
is more the proud
or tender flexing of feathers

outside the lexicon and learned
as water drinks reflection.

HEART SURGERY

My right leg slung over that elegant notch
where your hip rises
canted like a western saddle,

your head parked so your ear
makes a sharp, fossil impression
in the soft of my arm,

while our more primitive, forgotten feet
flipper innocently
at the bottom of the bed.

We are for now, a many armed goddess,
a bonne-bouche in the mouth of our planet.
We are while we can,

the biological knot of a new creature
brought forward from Kells
and our multi-chambered heart

moves the breath of our blood
with such kindness
it could stop war and famine.

But printed through the DNA we share
is notice posted of that surgery
that will pare our ventricles apart.

Such elegant thrift, to let us drift with fallen winds
and ancient trace of sun.

TO THE FIELD OF REEDS
The heart is measured in a scale against the feather of truth
in the Egyptian Book of the Dead.

42 gods waiting,
a placard held up,
one for each sin.

My heart, fat, elderly, shabby,
surely deserves some credit for keeping on
keeping on?

Over there the Field of Reeds.
My heart gives a little shall-I-make-it? skip.
Your feather trembles. Ever since I said I'm a liar

and a coward and you said 'yes, but I love you'
I've borrowed your compass.
Now that 42 pairs of eyes

are sizing up my canopic heart,
measuring the equilibrium of the scales,
I need it.

OK, OK, myth and procrastination.
You know and I know the Field of Reeds
is nothing more or less

than a Sunday morning in our bed
while we can. But lend me your feather
and I'll look very hard for my own.

One feather on each side
– trimmed and steady
as she goes.

MORE FROM ARACHNE PRESS
www.arachnepress.com

POETRY

The Other Side of Sleep: Narrative Poems
ISBN: 978-1-909208-18-6
Long, narrative poems by contemporary voices, including Inua Elams, Brian Johnstone, and Kate Foley, whose title poem for the anthology was the winner of the 2014 *Second Light* Long Poem competition.

The Don't Touch Garden by Kate Foley
ISBN: 978-1-909208-19-3 (print)
ISBN: 978-1-909208-52-0 (audio)
A complex autobiographical collection of poems of doption and identity, from award-winning poet Kate Foley.

With Paper for Feet by Jennifer A McGowan
ISBN: 978-1-909208-35-3
Poetry exploring myth and folklore.

Foraging by Joy Howard
ISBN: 978-1-909208-39-1
Poems of nature, human nature and grief, time and memory.

Erratics by Cathy Bryant (April 2018)
ISBN: 978-1-909208-56-8 Quirky poems of life, love and trouble.

LGBT

Outcome: LGBT Portraits by Tom Dingley
ISBN: 978-1-909208-26-1
80 full colour photographic portraits of LGBT people with the attributes of their daily life – and a photograph of themselves as a child. @OutcomeLGBT

The Dowry Blade by Cherry Potts
ISBN: 979-1-909208-20-9
When nomad Brede finds a wounded mercenary and the Dowry Blade, she is set on a journey of revenge, love, and loss.